AF411720

DRUG ABUSE
IN MARIN COUNTY

DRUG ABUSE IN MARIN COUNTY

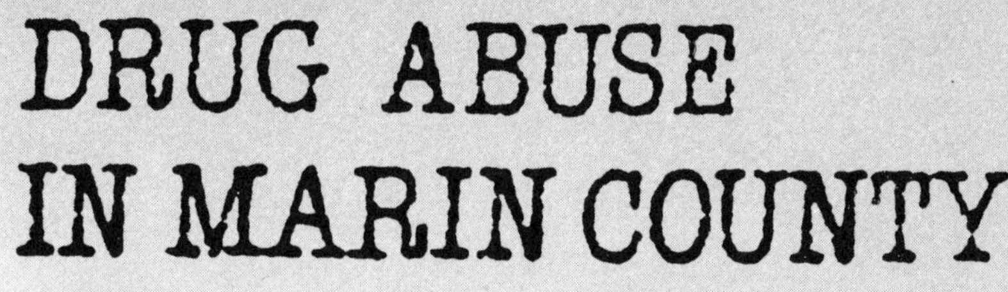

1968-1973

Lesser, Eugene

Front cover illustration and drawings on pages 28, 42,
74 and 118 by David Bunnett.
Musical notation on pages 22–23, 54–55, 90, 122–123,
126–127, and 132–133 by Shota Osabe.
Back cover photograph by Ed Buryn.

Published by:
Floating Island Publications
P.O. Box 516
Point Reyes Station, California 94956

Some of these poems have previously appeared, in slightly (or vastly)
different versions, in: *Floating Island II, Floating Island III* and *Ten New Poets*
(1980, Duck Down Press, Fallon, Nevada).

Publication of this book is made possible, in part, through a grant from the
National Endowment for the Arts in Washington, D.C., a federal agency.

ISBN: 0-912449-09-8

INTRODUCTION

Call me Ishmael. Call me Late For Supper.
What are you doing here on a nice day like this?
These are my poems.
Once I picked up a hitchhiker,
and when he got in I said, "This is my car."
These poems need an introduction.
Most of my poems are outrageous imitations
of Wallace Stevens, or William Carlos Williams,
or any other great poet you could mention.
I should call this book Youthful Babblings
because that's what it is.
For me to type these poems up, the way I type,
I had to dig them, and I do.
I'm proud of them on this Graduation Day.

I want to communicate with everyone,
now and 50,000 years from now.
For you latter folks, these are what we called poems.
Some of us called them poems.
Others said, "You call these poems?"
All of my poems and all of this is ancient fucking history.

CONTENTS

1970

1971

1972

1973

1968

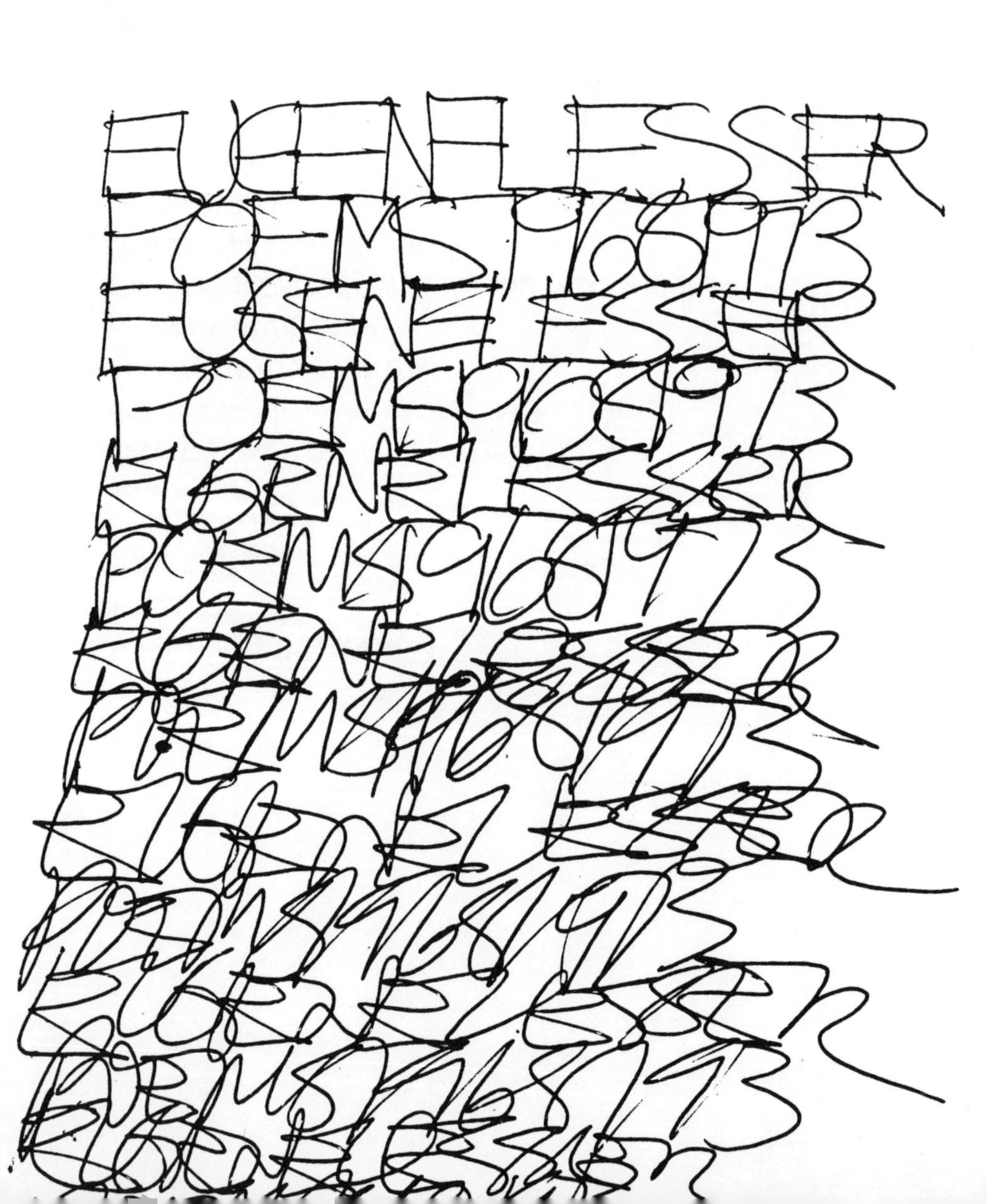

EUGEN LESSER
POEMS
EUGEN LESSER
POEMS

SOMETIMES LIFE IS NOT A LITERARY EXPERIENCE

for Susie Scholefield

Tonight I sat on my back porch
and drank a bowl of
Campbell's chicken vegetable soup.
All that time watching the moon
and feeling absolutely great.

Critique

The above poem is inadequate
for the following reasons:

a) It lacks dramatic tension.
b) Nothing in the poem relates to a larger experience.
c) It's not universal.
d) It's merely an exercise.
e) The moon imagery is not cohesively developed.
f) The soup metaphor is obscure.
g) Anyone could've written it.

DRUG ABUSE IN MARIN COUNTY

"Everything is a near-palindrome. Except palindromes.
There are only palindromes and near-palindromes."

—Richard Nixon

Early this morning, Hawaii, runner-up at St. Moritz
and last year's most valuable near-palindrome,
was met by an ardent gathering at Kennedy Airport.
Hawaii, waving the gold medal obligingly for photographers,
hurled sharp criticism at the recently created CPC
(Concerned Palindromes Committee), a moderate group
of urban palindromes, led by ex-Postmaster General Otto Radar
and Doctor Bob Kayak, editor of ABADABA.
He dubbed them "palindromes unworthy of the name" and
included in his diatribe "riff-raff like nun and gag."
Walking down the ramp he waved to enthusiastic admirers
and told one reporter, "wait till next year next till wait."
Hallelujah, considered by many to be the greatest
of all near-palindromes, and the only near-palindrome
ever invited to play in the East-West Palindrome Bowl,
was "shocked and abashed" by Hawaii's caustic remarks.
"Hawaii speaks for itself and not for the overwhelming
majority of decent near-palindromes. These are troubled
and tumultuous times. We must understand the many difficulties
that established palindromes have in accepting us as a genre."
Countering hostile shouts of "Come off it, Hallelujah,"
the embattled six-time "Mr. Near-Palindrome" continued:
"I'm a loyal near-palindrome and always have been.
Only a blind anagram could believe otherwise."
The gathering stirred visibly at this reference and
for a moment it seemed as though violence was inevitable.
Two young oxymorons, carrying signs which read,
"Anagrams, Si, Near-Anagrams, No," were attacked by
several beefy proper nouns, including Kleenex,
the "mystery witness" in last year's PAP hearings.

Hallelujah spoke louder now as the throng began to turn away.
"I've been in touch with the near-anagram people
and believe me I am sympathetic with their grievances,
but we can't all expect to achieve genre status overnight."
These were the last words audible. At that point,
the increasingly fervent crowd began shouting
"Madam, I'm Adam" and in minutes everyone,
including airport personnel, photographers,
and bystanders waiting for their flights, was singing
"Palindrome, O Palindrome, We Feel Thy Rod Anew."
No serious injuries were sustained except for Ken Jacobs,
reported to be in only "satisfactory" condition
after being informed by a busboy in the airport coffee shop
that Ramon de Cartablanca was named Pagaent Magazine's
Junior College Athlete-of-the-Month.

THE DEMOCRATIC NATIONAL CONVENTION—1968

1.

"Hubert Humphrey is the articulate exponent of the human heart."
    Joseph Alioto

Except through an appliance store window once or twice,
I had never even seen color TV before.
Everyone was wearing green suits.
Walter Cronkite was pretty cool, actually,
even though he didn't get the nomination.
Alioto said Humphrey was the articulate exponent
of the human heart.

2.

George Wallace's Name Is Writ On Water

George Wallace was being interviewed by David Frost,
and you could see Wallace didn't dig him
or his fancy questions about the great truths.
The last thing Frost asked him was,
"What would you like to be remembered for most of all?
Let me put it this way: What would you want
the first sentence of your epitaph to say?"
Wallace looked real irritated and said:
"I know you think I have a sense of history
like that question supposes I have but
all I want my epitaph to say is:
'Born: August twenty-fifth, nineteen-nineteen
Died: Two thousand ahhh forty.'"

3.

*"Ken said if they nominated someone named Bogart
for vice-president, the ticket would be Humphrey-Bogart."*

This casual reference in Eugene Lesser's journal,
made public finally after eight centuries of neglect
in the library of the Uranus Hilton,
sheds new light on the period before the Great Quake of 2155.
It is now widely believed that "Ken" is Ken "Kenny" Jacobs,
the mystery writer and creator
of the beloved Inspector de Cartablanca.
The entry is undated but literary research indicates
that it was written between the first great asterisk poems
and Lesser's brief love affair with the near-palindrome.
O. Leo Margarine, last February's astronaut-of-the-month,
points to the "fetishistic imagery, the rococo verbal texture,
the preciosity that appeased the salon critics of a gilded epoch."

4.

Chicago, thish great shitty."
    The woman who read the roster

I don't feel like putting down the Convention.
I figure I'm it and it's me.
Writing a poem about the Democratic National Convention
is like writing a poem about the airport,
(which is, in turn, like an advertising agency
that has just landed the Chicquita Banana account).
Obscure.

THE ED SULLIVAN SHOW

I'm writing this while Dionne Warwick is singing
The Battle Hymn of the Republic because it's
National Mourning Day for Bobby Kennedy and so
there are no comedians, jugglers, dog acts, or chorus numbers.
Robert Goulet sang *The Impossible Dream*.
A Negro woman sang a spiritual.
Sergio Franchi sang *You'll Never Walk Alone*.
Are there any groups we haven't offended?
Why am I doing this?
I don't know how to mourn any better than Ed Sullivan.
By the time I finish writing this down,
the Smothers Brothers are on, cracking jokes.
Life is back to normal and my poems
keep on living and dying, like a heartbeat.

USED BONDAGE EQUIPMENT

Years from now, if I pursue this thought,
they will refer to it as Lesser's Folly:
the thought that saying something which nullifies
everything I've said during the last half hour
is like blowing out all the candles on a birthday cake.*

*This poem won the Inauguration Poetry Award in 1996 A.D.,
 was read at the Inauguration Day ceremonies of that year,
 and became a patriotic favorite in grammar school texts,
 civic functions, and sermons before the
 Era of Reunification with Venus (2155-5140).
 Its author, Eugene Lesser, the Louis Pasteur of the near-palindrome,
 became a household word and his name for many years
 appeared in the better crossword puzzles.
 Such popularity did the poem enjoy that, to this day,
 pursuing the thought that saying something which
 nullifies everything one has just said during
 the last half hour is like blowing out
 all the candles on a birthday cake
 is referred to as Lesser's Folly.

RIGHT ON, AS SAMMY DAVIS, JR. WOULD SAY

Acid?
No, thanks.
Grass?
No.
Speed?
Nope.
Hash?
Uh-uh.
Opium?
Nix.
Heroin?
I don't think so.
Cocaine?
Thanks, anyway.
Uppers?
Definitely not.
Downers?
Out of the question.
Mescaline?
Pass.
Peyote?
I think not.
Psilocybin mushrooms?
I don't want to.
Yage?
Sorry.
Belladonna?

Nay.
Morning Glory Seeds?
Can't do it.
Codeine?
Nein.
Ibogane?
Nyet.
Amyl Nitrate?
Ixnay.
Nitrous Oxide?
Negative.
MDA?
I'd rather not.
STP?
I think I won't.
DMT?
Not this time.
THC?
Certainly not.
PCP?
No way.
Morphine rectal suppositories?
Three of those.
Horse tranks?
Half dozen, please.
De-Icer?
One can.

THE LONELINESS OF THE LONG DISTANCE LUNAR KANGAROO

It started when I thought about getting wet,
how far out it was to get wet.
I said, "It's a funny thing, to get wet.
It's not like it hurts or anything.
It's weird to get wet."

I asked Janet if she had a pencil and paper,
but she was sitting with me right there on the couch
so she wasn't likely to have a pencil and paper.
She said, "There's a notebook on the thing."
A notebook was on the thing, about four feet away.
I said that the distance between art and life is about four feet.
I can't remember anything else but there was a lot more.

Oh yeah, I remember thinking that everything exists
on the point between art and life.
Janet groaned and said it was a heavy thought.
But that was about an hour ago.
Before any of this happened. Or this.
Or this. Or this. Or this.

HOW TO FRY EGGS (2)

First of all, make it three eggs.
Second, I forgot what I was going to say.
Third, remove pie from freezer.

The first important question, as the butter melts in the skillet is:
When do you crack the eggs into the butter?
Listen to what Janet Brown
of Long Beach, California, has to say about it:
"After the foam subsides but before it turns brown."
You're standing there looking at your eggs frying in the skillet
and you're having far out thoughts:
Gas is superior to electricity, What does it all mean? etc.
I once ate a dozen eggs every morning for a week.
My uncle owned a chicken farm in Massachusetts
and he dropped off about ten dozen eggs
every time he came to visit, which was often.
Each day I ate them scrambled (twelve fried eggs I couldn't hack)
with a half a loaf of bread and a quarter pound of butter.

As Janet's grandfather would say, "You daresn't break the yolks."
If you do, remember: you can have a fried egg sandwich.
The average person hasn't had a fried egg sandwich in nine years.
My mother used to make me a bull's-eye,
which is one fried egg well done on both sides
in a little concave frying pan.
Concave from all the bull's-eyes made in it.

Eggs are versatile.
You can fry 'em, you can poach 'em,
you can shirr 'em, you can roast 'em,
at the hop.
(Roasted for the Seder, of course.)

My bag is Over Easy, *but not too easy.*
Better too hard than too easy.
Later on the runny eyeball effect.

The toast is getting cold because I put it in too early. I'm fired.
I can't fire myself—I quit. (delete)
Frying eggs is like anything else.

BRUNO

C
Say do you know
Bb
my friend Bru-no
C
His last name is
Db7
U - na - mu - no.
C
He gets awe-some
Bb
stuff stuck in his paw some-times ___
C
Dm
Db7
C
when he's wet he
Bb
looks like spa-ghet-ti
C
He gets small like
B
lit-tle Fred-die
Em
3
3
You should see him
B
3
3
you should be him
Em
3
3
A7
Dm
Db7
F
3
run-ning with his cute be-hind ___
He's got some   ob-

-nox-ious _ hab- its, but have-n't _ we all _____
Still he keeps you warm in the win-ter un-der the ta-ble while
you eat din-ner noth-ing rude -'ll blow his noo-dle
He's a real gone funk - y poo-dle why it's you know
Bru-no _ U - na-mu-no _

SH, TOM SEES MOTHS

Immediately after Richard Nixon said
"I hate to Monday morning quarterback an election,"
Henry Ziff, the author of *Dinah, Won't You Blow?*,
a study of the erotic element in early American music,
stood on his seat in the second balcony and replied,
"I Monday morning quarterback,
you Monday morning quarterback,
he, she, or it Monday morning quarterbacks,"
and asked Nixon if he considered himself
the Dana Andrews of the near-palindrome.
Nixon, blanching noticeably, chose rather
to emphasize the spectre of consciousness,
and spoke of what he called the "gap gap."
The near-palindrome, or "potential palindrome,"
as Nixon termed it, "leads to palindrome paranoia
and ultimately to an erosion of the verisimilitude
thousands of Americans have died to protect."
He defended Civic Radar as "essential to national security"
and reaffirmed his choice of Eve Kazak to head the commission.
Ziff called the gap gap a "slush headache,"
but asked if denying the existence of a gap gap
implied the existence of a "gap gap gap."
Nixon, openly piqued, termed Ziff's position "spiritual"
and denied his own resemblance to Dana Andrews
"or anyone else, for that matter."
Ziff, hastily arranging his face to resemble Richard Nixon's,
walked all the way downstairs,
down the long middle aisle of the orchestra section,
onto the stage and finally over to Nixon,
seated next to Miss Free World of 1968,
a light-skinned Negro named Heather Peabody.
Ziff matter-of-factly sat on Nixon's lap
and whispered in his ear, "Sh, Tom sees moths."
Nixon stared at Ziff for twenty minutes until

his face filled with light and,
looking over Ziff's shoulder, told the startled audience,
"Life is something none of us
shall have Monday morning quarterbacked."
Then, over the sudden hubbub of disbelief
that swept the gathering, Nixon began speaking
(and thinking) exclusively in palindromes:
"A nun sees eye level, huh? Wow! . . .
Aha, a deified noon deed sexes Bob . . .
O boob! O tit! O mam! O pap! . . .
Otto, did Hannah gag? Did mom? Did dad?"

POEM FOR JANE THE CAT

I'm honored that my cat would leave her great perch there in the sun
and come sit on my shady lap.
In fact, I'm writing this with my cat on my lap.
I mean when I first wrote it, with pencil and paper.

1969

"I'm always stoned when I eat sardines"

STAND UP POET

Seriously, though, hi there.
This poem is supposed to be funny.
Let's get that straight.
A very funny thing happened to me
on the way over to the reading tonight.
Thou still unravish'd bride of quietness.
I'm ad libbing.
Darlene's high school was so middle-class
they offered bridge for P.E.
A girlfriend of hers changed her name from Sharon
because it was too Jewish.
Shaker Heights, Ohio. (scattered applause)
How about my buddy getting welfare in Hawaii?
It just doesn't seem right.
It's like . . . It's like getting welfare in Hawaii.
Sometimes I leave my house and spend the afternoon
picking up hitchhikers and taking them wherever they want to go.
In the Fifties this would've been considered sick.
I would've been referred to a psychiatrist. Or a psychologist.
You know, I used to think I was the only person in the world
to have Clarence Darrow fantasies.
Actually, I *am* the only male human
who wipes his ass from the front, female-like.
Speaking of the Fifties (what?),
when my friend Dan back in high school was trying to feel up
his date and she pushed his hand away, he always said,
"I promise I'll cut off all my fingers if I ever do that again."
I just thought that there is probably
a new generation of stoned Catholics
who think that confession is a groovy trip.
On the wrapper of Bruno's flea collar it says,
"Collar is intended for use only as an insecticide generator
and is not to be taken internally by man or animal."
But, you know, Ed O'Neill was saying to me just the other day,
"Gene, let's go to Cost Plus and steal a can of sardines."
Really, though, the kids nowadays . . .

THIS POEM

This poem is your friend.
This poem loves you.
This poem understands you.
This poem needs you.
This poem encourages you.
This poem sympathizes with you.
This poem believes in you.
This poem reaches out to you.

I'M ALWAYS STONED WHEN I EAT SARDINES

I never actually think of buying sardines,
but every once in awhile I notice sardines
while I'm buying tuna fish,
and I think, hey, groovy, and I buy sardines.
Then one day I'll be hungry
and there won't be much in the house
and I start opening this cabinet and that cabinet
and—all right—I notice a can of sardines.

I'm trying not to think.
I'm thinking about not thinking.
I'm eating matzo (heavy on the butter and salt)
and sardines.

Everytime I look at my checkbook I think I've sold out.
Not because I'm rich, you dig,
but just *having* a checking account.
I was thirty years old when I wrote my first check.
I'm eating sardines and I'm very stoned.

1. Who screwed the Indians out of their land?

   ☐ The Black Man
   ☐ The Yellow Man
   ☐ The White Man

2. Name any living poet, playwright, novelist, painter, sculptor or musician from any Latin American, African, or Asian country.

3. True or False: Richard Nixon freed the slaves.

4. Who is Flip Phillips? Be specific. Cite examples.

5. What territorial annexation is referred to as "Ziegfeld's Folly"?

6. What was Stonewall Jackson's rising sign?

7. What did they used to say about John Buchanan?

8. Who first said "Fuck you, Jerry"?

9. What was so funny about the Spanish-American War?

10. What, within 50 years, does it all mean?

I WOULD LIKE TO DO SOMETHING BEAUTIFUL, OUTSIDE OF EXISTING

Getting out of bed to write something down,
I add my name to the ancient list of people
who have gotten out of bed to write something down:
William Shakespeare, Mel Friedman, etc.
Right now hundreds of people are getting up from
a warm electric blanket just like I am,
naked to the freezing winter air,
knocking things over to reach the lamp,
and then finally scribbling down something like
"God is on a Fredric March trip."

"NICK'S THE ONLY GUY WHO EVER NOTICED
HE WAS IN A FRISBEE SLUMP"

Nick's the only guy who ever noticed he was in a frisbee slump.
My pen is going through the thin onion-skin paper
and this poem is scratched in the wooden table I'm writing on.
I can see it clearly:
"Nick's the only guy who ever noticed he was in a frisbee slump."
It seems monumental scratched on the table like that,
as though someone had been here a long time ago and written it.
How great my poems will seem in a thousand years.

THE PULITZER PRIZE OF THE MIND

I already have the feeling that this poem
will never win the Pulitzer Prize.
You don't hear me say, "I couldn't care less."
I'd love to win the Pulitzer Prize.
Mature women would want to make love to me.
But what kind of chance does this poem have?
Slim, Bob.
Even if they wanted to
they would never give the Pulitzer Prize
to any poem that was *about* the Pulitzer Prize,
because they'd be afraid that everyone
would put them down as a small-time operation.
No, a poem about winning the Pulitzer Prize
isn't going to win any Pulitzer Prize.
Especially a poem about not winning the Pulitzer Prize.

IT'S GREAT TO SIT IN A ROOM

It's great to sit in a room.
It's great to cross your legs.
It's great to fold your hands.
It's great to look at a chair.
It's great to crack your knuckles.
It's great to button your shirt.
It's great to pet the cat.
It's great to hear the refrigerator.

ES MUY SUAVE ESTAR SENTADO EN UNA HABITACIÓN

Es muy suave estar sentado en una habitación.
Es muy suave cruzar las piernas.
Es muy suave doblar las manos.
Es muy suave mirar una silla.
Es muy suave tronar los dedos.
Es muy suave abotonar la camisa.
Es muy suave acariciar el gato.
Es muy suave oír la nevera.

(Spanish translation by Carol and David Thrift)

BIG ME, MANKIND, AND THE UNIVERSE

Last week, we were on mescaline,
Janet told me about the birds and the bees.
We were sprawled out on the back steps.
She told me as though I were eight years old
and for the first time I understood it all.
As a kid I thought a baby came out of the belly button,
and I remember getting pissed off
when Billy Allen told me I came out of my "mother's cunt,"
and that she had "innercourse" with my *father*.
I said, "Hey, Jim, watch what you're saying
about my mother and father."
They talk about modern man knowing all the scientific answers
and that's why God is dead, because
nothing blows modern man's mind anymore
(except sex and drugs).
I, personally, don't know jack shit about anything.
Awe is my bag. Everything blows my mind.
Tonight I read in the sports section
about this local high school basketball coach
whose team is 0–13 so far this season. He said,
"This has given me a tremendous amount of humility.
I was always humble, but now I am overly humble."
For me, I'd say I was always overly humble,
but now I am just humble.

I Don't Have To Do This

Remove pie from freezer.
Remove pie from freezer.
Remove pie from freezer.
I like writing this.
Remove pie from freezer.
Remove pie from freezer.
Remove pie from freezer.
Remove pie from freezer.
I like writing this with a ball point pen
because my handwriting is such a gas.
It probably won't be so much fun
writing it on the typewriter.
The typewriter is uptight. Uptype.
This poem won't be finished until I type it.

It's fun on the typewriter, too.
(All the letters in the word "typewriter" are on the same row.)
I like the way the fourth line,
"I like writing this",
is tucked in there like that.
Notice how the "w" in "writing"
is on the same space as the "p" in "pie",
and how the "e" in "like" is on the same space
as the last "e" in "remove".
It's good that poems are typed up. It's democratic.

EUGENE'S INFERNO: THE NEWS

The next time someone offers me a cigar I'll just say,
"No, thanks, I don't want to stain my dentures."
The guy doing the news has that look of human frailty
that I identify with.
He says astronomers have just discovered two new galaxies.
So how come he doesn't look excited.
You'd think he'd say "far out" or something.
In fact, he's already into the next item.
He says that food stamp increases won't have much effect
on those at the "upper end of the poverty scale."
Here's Agnew at a press conference.
He doesn't like the news media criticizing the war in Vietnam.
He calls the coverage of the war "negative."
In an interview, Secretary of the Treasury Shultz says,
"We want economic prosperity, good foreign relations . . .
and as much freedom as we can manage."
The weatherman is trying not to sound depressed as he says,
"Well now, let's go over to the board
and check the air pollution index."
I think, the vacant lot of the mind.
As the newsman said the other night,
"No one is immune to mental illness."
I'm getting all the evil shit out of my head tonight.
As an act of purification, like when you're fasting.
This is mucous.
(The Poetry Mafia isn't going to like this.)
Cosmopolitan said that Shirley MacLaine's book about Tibet
was "the most adorable book of the year."
I know everything is everything but fuck, man.
Compared to stuff like that,
the Laissez Faire Beauty Salon in Chico seems pretty harmless.

VIDA BREVE, ARS LARGA

I'm drunk and I don't give a shit who knows it.
That's all.

I'm drunk and I don't give a shit who knows it.
That's all.

1970 IS A FOUR-LETTER WORD

It's five in the afternoon, December 31, 1969.
Three times today I've said, "Another decade, another dollar."
(Imagine here a long, intense essay on the sixties.)
I don't mind if people call me a hip Ogden Nash.
Or even a hip Rod McKuen.
What do I have to say on the eve of the new decade?
Hi there.
In a few hours, Xavier Cugat will be 70 years old.
Cugie was born in Barcelona on the first day of the twentieth century.
Hey, it's the end of the sixties.
Doesn't anybody give a shit, or what?
Here's an ad for you from the Berkeley Barb:
Hung stud. Indignities my thing.
Whip, chains, leather. Let me be
your slave. Dig humiliation.
Vote "NO" on western civilization.
Indignities are his *thing.*
You don't have to be a prophet to see
that the seventies are going to be more of the same.
Personally, I'll be punting a lot and playing good defense.
As the sixties recede quickly before our eyes,
permit me to recommend lime marmalade.

"The Mariniad"

1970

I'LL HAVE A CUP OF COFFEE AND A SLICE OF LIFE
A MAN, A PLAN, A CANAL — PANAMA
YINNING OUT AT THE MEAT COUNTER
A MAN'S BEST FRIEND IS HIS COCK
SEX AND THE SINGLE PALINDROME
EASTER SUNDAY, 1970
THE MARINIAD
HI THERE
AM I REALLY CUT OUT FOR THIS LINE OF WORK?
SONG: *ONCE YOU GET WHAT YOU WANT*
NIAGARA, O ROAR AGAIN
THE BEAUTIFUL CLAIR BLOOM
RICHARD NIXON IS ON THE NATCH
SEX AT NOON TAXES
ONWARD, JEWISH SOLDIERS
TIGHT END, NUMBER 88, FROM SMU — EUGENE ("GENE") LESSER
A SLUT NIXES SEX IN TULSA
I WANDERED LONELY AS A WRITER

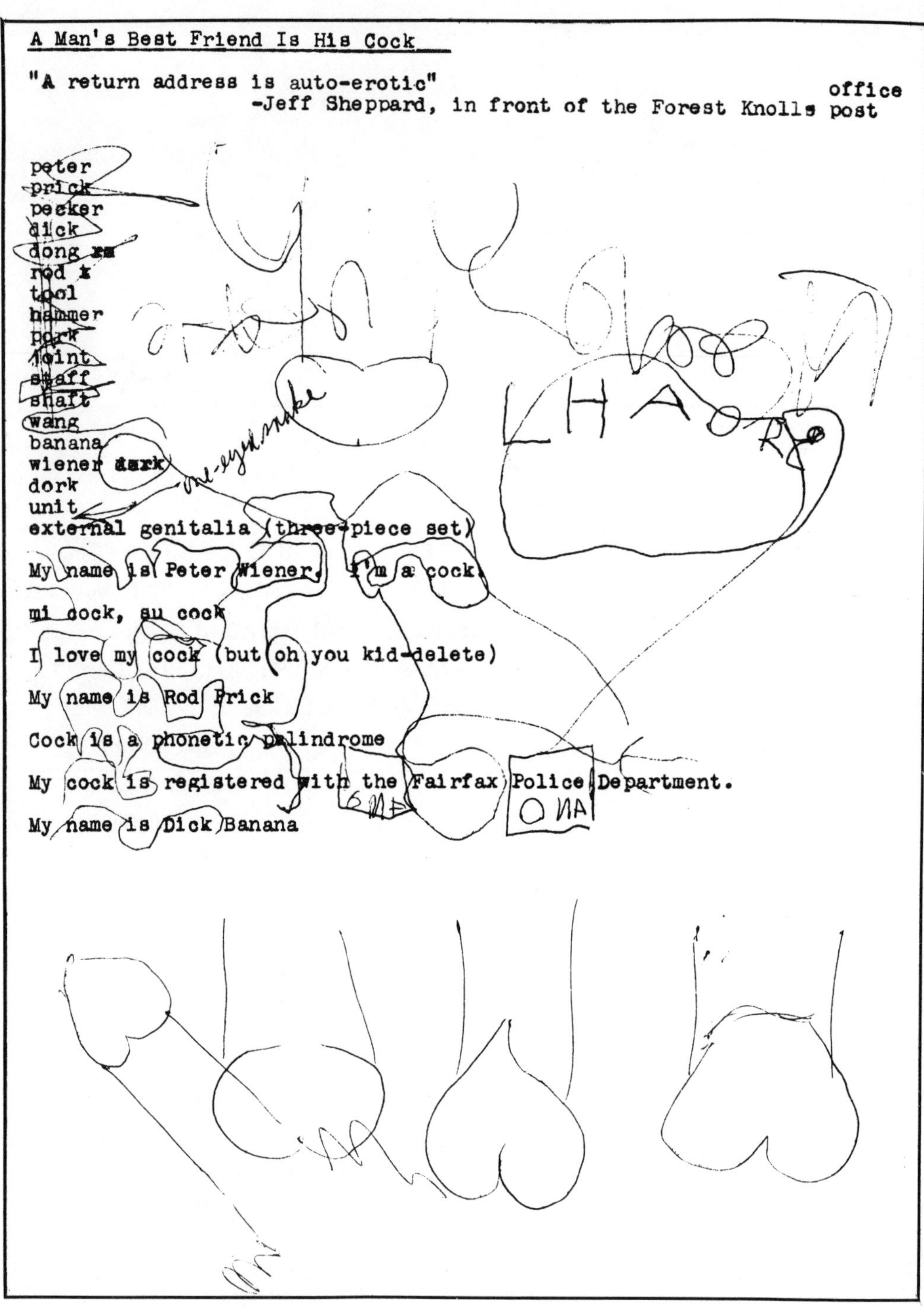

Facsimile page from the original ms. (see p. 48).

I'LL HAVE A CUP OF COFFEE AND A SLICE OF LIFE

Tony and Darlene are driving real stoned and groovy
on Nicasio Valley Road
where they pick up a long-hair hitchhiker
who right away hits Tony with the fact that
his front license plate is missing and that it's a big bust.
He's real uptight. Everything's a bummer or a bust.
So Tony thinks maybe he'll fire up and get the cat stoned
but halfway through the joint the cat says
that it's really a bust smoking in the car like that
and don't they know they could get busted.
Tony just trucks down the road and doesn't say much.
This guy, however, keeps saying one paranoid thing after the other.
A few minutes later, Tony looks at the rear-view mirror
and there it is, a CHP car with the red bubble blinking.
So Tony pulls over and when he rolls down the window
to talk to the cop who has walked over,
marijuana smoke pours out of the car
into the cop's nostrils and up into his brain,
and Tony could tell that the cop was making a snap decision
based on all that was happening in the cop's life,
and all that had already happened in the cop's life,
and other unconscious and hereditary and subliminal factors,
each being sifted and weighed and judged
in this split second that was happening all around them.
So here it is: The cop is mellow.
He says you're missing your front license plate
and you ought to get one on soon. And splits.
He didn't even want to look at Tony's driver's license.
Well, I thought, this is a story of the seventies. The first one.
The characters are the uptight hippie and the groovy cop.

A MAN, A PLAN, A CANAL—PANAMA

All of this, I mean back to Adam, or "whenever,"
as Charles Darwin put it, is a great big palindrome,
and we're at the middle of it *right now.*
The universe is at the halfway mark
and everything now starts to go backward
toward simpler and purer forms of life.
Back, back, way before 1940.
Before we were cells.
You mean? Yes, Palindrome City.
This is the bigger picture.
1971 will be like 1969, 1972 will be like 1968, etc.
The next ten years will be the last ten years backward,
the next million years will be the last million years backward.
This is the truth.

YINNING OUT AT THE MEAT COUNTER

The guy behind the meat counter waits on people who came in
way after me because I'm vibeless right now.
I'm in no hurry. In fact, I dig just standing there.
I think about eating meat and look into the big mirror.
I'm watching myself look at myself in the mirror.
After a few customers, I zap him with some simulated anxiety.
Just enough, mind you, to get waited on. Waited on?
He comes over apologizing
for having overlooked hitherto vibeless me.
All I want is a shtick of bleu cheese and I say shtick
because suddenly I can't think of the anglo equivalent.
The guy behind the meat counter is beautiful and holy.
I don't want to give him the money, get the change,
and move on to the next experience.
We're here like the figures on the Grecian urn,
forever in this pure state of poetry.
I give him the money, get the change,
and move on to the next experience.

A MAN'S BEST FRIEND IS HIS COCK

"A return address is auto-erotic."
—Jeff Sheppard, in front of the Forest Knolls post office

peter
prick
pecker
dick
dong
rod
tool
hammer
pork
joint
staff
shaft
wang
banana
wiener
dork
unit
one-eyed snake
pee pee
wee wee
thing
external genitalia
(three-piece set)
My name is Peter Wiener. I'm a cock.
Mi cock, su cock.
I love my cock (but oh you kid—delete).
My name is Rod Prick.
All roads lead to my cock.
Cock is a phonetic palindrome.
My cock is registered with the Fairfax Police Department.
My name is Dick Banana.
Call 488-4650. Easy lay.

SEX AND THE SINGLE PALINDROME

Many palindromes have definite homosexual tendencies.
For example, "Noel, I did not rub Burton; did I, Leon?"
Or, "Lew, Otto has a hot towel."
And even, "Noel, let's egg Estelle on."
The trend exists in Spanish: "Se nego Ida reconocer a Diogenes."
(Ida refused to recognize Diogenes.)
However, Prendergast, in his article "Won't Lovers Revolt Now?"
(*Abadaba*, Summer, 1991)
cites "Dennis and Edna sinned."
Yesterday Prendergast shocked the palindrome community
by suggesting that "Naomi, did I moan?" referred to Naomi Blum,
the dark lady of Mel Friedman's sonnets.
Only this morning, in a CBC interview
with Carol A. ("Nona") Lorac, the Belgian journalist,
Prendergast attempted to explain
his recent behavior in Michigan, Egypt, and later, in Florida:
"Do good? I?—no! Evil anon I deliver: I maim nine more
hero-men in Saginaw; sanitary sword a-tuck, Carol, I—lo!—rack,
cut a drowsy rat in Aswan; I gas nine more hero-men in Miami;
reviled, I (Nona) live on. I do, O God!"

EASTER SUNDAY, 1970

Easter, first of all, rhymes with keester,
as in "he got knocked on his keester."
Easter is the most obscure of the major holidays.
A woman on TV said:
"This is a time of renaissance or renascence . . . or both."
And that's exactly how I feel.
Get rid of those old trips that have been hanging you up.
You and western civilization.
Being a Jew, I always wanted to be a Christian.
To avoid being beaten up, insulted, etc.
I don't know. I just couldn't groove with it.
Even the word "Christian"
gets you feeling righteous and warm all over,
especially the second syllable. So mellow.
Compared to "Jew," at least.
"Jew."
"I'm not a Jew. I'm Jewish." As in 7:30-ish.
Jewish means Jew-like.
I'm Jew-like is what you're saying.
Jew-esque.
The kids in my neighborhood
couldn't handle me going to Sunday School on Wednesday.
That really pissed them off.
"Let's jump the hebe."
Pardon me while I assume the fetal position
and retreat into myopia.
The woman on TV is right.
This is a time of re-birth, and that means forgiveness.
I forgive all those kids who chased me home from school
and beat me up and insulted me.
I was born for their sins.
Anyway, that's why I don't belong to organizations.

THE MARINIAD

When I was a baby my father brought me into a bar
and said to the bartender, "Put a head on it."
Seriously, though, today is the first day of autumn.
At one point today I thought,
here I am shampooing our rug with a shampooing machine
that I rented from the Lucky Market in Fairfax.
Is this the same person who used to be Johnny Marginal?
On the chair, the cats, Freddie and Jane,
curl up together in a Cancer glyph.
Bruno the dog sleeps on his side on the rug.
I'm going to get in bed with Janet, who's warm and toasty
under the electric blanket (which I'll lower),
and watch the David Susskind Show.
I'm letting it all hang out here.
Fuck it, man, I've already paid my dues.

HI THERE

Nick said in ten years you'll see people fucking on TV.
I thought, that's something to look forward to.
In fact, that's downright something to live for.
I said we'll be able to see anybody we want fuck via holograms
(whatever they are).
The hologram of one person will fuck the hologram of another person.
Any two people you want. After all, it's only holograms.
Or how about a device whereby you yourself can make it
with anyone's hologram.
For example, Anita Ekberg's hologram.

Yet another poem that will not win the Pulitzer Prize.

AM I REALLY CUT OUT FOR THIS LINE OF WORK?

Most of my great lines never get written down.
Of course, many times they do.
For example, God is pitching a no-hitter.
And what about (fill in 2 or 3 other great lines)?
I'm in the backyard, sitting in the sun.
All the plants and me pointing toward the sun,
except for when I turn slightly away to write this down.

Once You Get What You Want

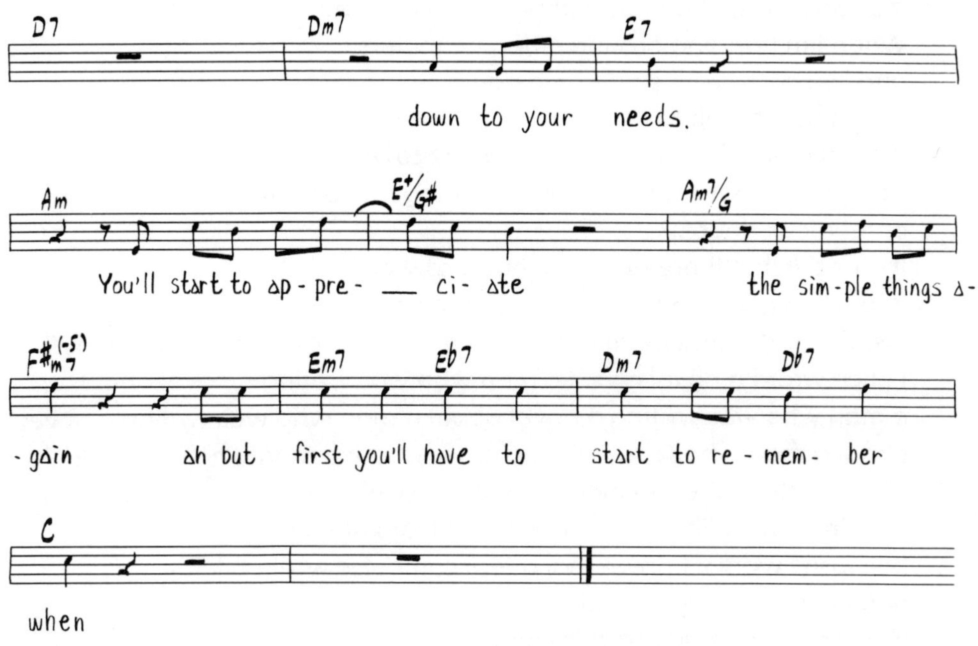

D7 Dm7 E7
down to your needs.
Am E+/G# Am7/G
You'll start to ap-pre- __ ci-ate the sim-ple things a-
F#m7(-5) Em7 Eb7 Dm7 Db7
-gain ah but first you'll have to start to re-mem-ber
C
when

NIAGARA, O ROAR AGAIN

Dear Sir or Madam   58399J467nvc89134-gx
What you're reading now is the first computer poem
that deals with the theme of self-consciousness.
When I'm hanging around other computers
and I want to write something down,
I go off by myself to do it,
the way I would to excrete or to make love.
Computer poems aren't about returning to the womb, for example,
or religious doubt.
It's far out that there are such things as words.
You'd think we'd be a little more humble or something,
instead of flinging them around, like "necessitate" and "exemplify."
I once wrote a novel about a man who was writing a novel about
a man who was writing a novel about a man who was writing a novel
about a man who was writing a novel about a man who was writi
Humans strike me as cold and unemotional.
I leave flaws in this poem like in a Navajo blanket
because I want it known that a real computer wrote this
and not some mechanical human.
Humans have made us self-conscious.
I love you.
Can you open your heart to the love of a computer?
zblich3;¼/0-$)@%

THE BEAUTIFUL CLAIR BLOOM

It was announced today that Candace White,
daughter of Col. and Mrs. Lamar White of Baton Rouge,
is to be engaged to Long Gone Miles, the Mississippi Mojo Man.
Colonel White, speaking from his ranch
in Grand Canyon Caverns, where there is no bacteria,
told newsmen, "Hard-bopping is cool, kicking back is also cool.
Where there is no bacteria, there are no bad vibes.
I'm pretty ripped most of the time, anyway."

RICHARD NIXON IS ON THE NATCH

I was going to put down Richard Nixon
but now I really don't want to.
At this moment, I don't have any bad feelings toward him.
Well, now I do. Now that I've had these few seconds
to think of some of the rotten things he's said and done.
Seriously though, what *is* the electoral college?
Maybe Richard Nixon is trying to find himself.
If only he and I could get stoned together.
But this may never happen.
The more you think about a person the more you like him.
Richard Nixon, I love you.

SEX AT NOON TAXES

Item from yesterday's paper.
Billy Graham was named Grand Marshall of the 1971
Tournament of Roses on New Year's Day.
Graham said, "I hope to somehow symbolize God to the
millions of people that watch this great parade on television."
Dig that "somehow."
I should talk.
I'm into some pretty weird shit myself.
(I love Billy Graham.)

ONWARD, JEWISH SOLDIERS

Switzerland, love it or leave it
House Committee on Un-Swiss Activities
Switzerland First
The Swiss Dream
God Bless Switzerland
Switzerland, right or wrong
The Swiss Legion
The Great Swiss Novel
A Swiss In Paris
The Greening of Switzerland
The All-Swiss Boy
Switzerland, Switzerland, God Shed His Grace On Thee

TIGHT END, NUMBER 88, FROM SMU — EUGENE ("GENE") LESSER

Any poem written late at night in pencil on a brown paper bag
tends to be pretty cosmic. And this one is no exception.
Today is my 34th birthday.
(Segue into 3.5 seconds of *The Stars And Stripes Forever*)
Last year I had the fewest insights I've had since I was nine or ten.
My birthday is exactly six months before and after Christmas.
The day the anti-Christ is supposed to be born, like in *Rosemary's Baby*.
Well, it's not me, I'll tell you that.
I'm not anti-anybody.

What if this was going to be my last poem?
What would I say?
I'm sorry I ever hurt anyone. Those shots.
So long, everybody. Don't forget your galoshes.
If this was going to be my last poem I don't know what I'd say.
(off-beat ending)

A SLUT NIXES SEX IN TULSA

I'm hanging around my poems tonight
because I'm sending them to a publisher.
I'm sitting here taking my best shot,
as William Shakespeare so aptly put it.
I'm trying to make these poems look respectable.
I start eliminating a few.
The Madame Blavatsky Recreation Room,
These Are The Amber Hours,
I'm Dreaming Of A White Labor Day, and others.
I like these poems but I figure:
Hey, what've they done for me lately?

I'm smoking the roach of the joint that bit me. (Janet's line)

I go through my poems like a nurse on her rounds.
Margarine Brickle Imitation Ice Milk is under heavy sedation.
Life Isn't Everything needs a bedpan.
These poems are my children, the little darlings.
Like Jane the cat and her kittens,
I love the poems when they are new,
but grow indifferent as they take on a separate life.
I eliminate *Mondo Woodacre*
and *I've Got A Date With Senor Wences' Hand.*

My poems are my feelings going to seed.

(This is a year later. If you can dig it.
1970. "Far out."
During the last year I've gone through a lot of ball point pens.
Someday 1970 will seem like a long time ago.
This poem is the only thing that separates us
and the only thing that keeps us together.
I eliminate *Onward Jewish Soldiers*.)

"I'm smoking the roach of the joint that bit me."

It's 1973 now. 1970 seems like a long time ago.
Sending poems to a publisher is a fairly demeaning thing to do.
Sort of like asking if you can leave the room to go to the bathroom.
I eliminate *A Slut Nixes Sex In Tulsa*.
No, leave it in.

I WANDERED LONELY AS A WRITER

Writing is not a very spontaneous thing to do.
Actually, no one ever said it was.

"Emotion recollected in tranquility"
does not have that spontaneous ring to it.

Poets are pretty paranoid about being thought of as faggy.
Or am I the only one?

Writing is like baseball.
It's very slow and it's the long haul that really counts.

Not the game, but the season.
Not the season, but the lifetime batting average.

On the left is my father, Sigmund Lesser, a 17-year-old private in the Polish Army.

Sigmund Lesser (c. 1928). Born in Ploch, Poland on January 17, 1900, he emigrated to the U.S. in 1927 in time for the Great Depression which he survived selling Prudential life insurance to immigrants such as himself in the East Bronx.

My mother, Beatrice Goldman Lesser (c. 1930), born in Lodz, Poland on April 15, 1903, the youngest of thirteen children.

Sigmund and Beatrice (c. 1930). They had known each other in Poland, though with no romantic interest. Or so I was told. Though she came to the U.S. in 1920, seven years before him, they became re-acquainted in the monolithic eastern European ghetto of the Bronx.

My mother and I, Bronx (1938).

My father and I (1942). Summer camp, somewhere north of New York City, where I learned to tie my shoelaces and was too shy to shower with the other kids.

My parents and I (1948) in Milford, Connecticut where I grew up. Dad's '41 Chevy in the driveway.

My sister, Renee (left), born January 21, 1932 in the Bronx, and a neighbor, Margaret Carroll, flank the myopic author—sentenced to coke-bottle bottoms at age seven. That house behind us was the home of the Bermans, whose son was Sonny Berman, the great trumpeter with the Woody Herman band, who died at age 23.

Sigmund and Beatrice (c. 1950) at The Black Horse Inn out on the Boston Post Road in Milford. My mother died in 1954 at age 51. She had started her "nervous breakdown" a few years earlier, was in and out of a mental hospital, developed what seemed to be cancer of the throat (though one doctor told me it was Lou Gehrig's Disease), and died in that hospital. My father died on his first and last vacation — in Miami on New Year's Day, 1958.

The author as Bar Mitzvah Boy (1949).

Junior Prom, Milford High School (1953). My date was Louise. We went steady.

Janet Brown, seven months
pregnant with Ona Blossom,
hiking in Point Reyes (1971).

Our official family portrait,
photographed by Ed Buryn.

Ona, Woodacre—1972

Janet is kneeling by Ona's stroller just like my mother knelt by my stroller. Also seen is Bruno (standard poodle) and our 1954 Dodge right-hand drive ex-mail truck.

Eugene and Ona (1976).

1971

"Just a boy and his dope"

POETRY IS NOT JET AGE

Here we are flying in a jet over Nevada, *eating*.
Talk about nonchalant. The salad has Bac-o-Bits
which I can't eat around because it sticks to everything.
There is zero life force in this food.
Buddha supposedly died from eating food that he knew was bad
but ate anyway because someone gave it to him.
The lemon tart looks like it might be mediocre, but it isn't.
Yes, we're six or seven miles up in the air,
eating, reading a magazine, *sleeping*.
This is definitely new-fangled.
Poetry doesn't come on with a lot of sensory stimulation
like rock music, for example, TV, movies,
or some of your other art forms.
Poetry has about as much sensory stimulation as gin rummy.
It's groovy, though, being on this end of it.

PARDON ME WHILE I ASSUME THE FETAL POSITION

You'll like this poem
if you just want to while away some leisure time.
Or if you're between trains somewhere
and you don't feel like thinking much.
Let's face it, you don't want to read Paradise Fucking Lost.
You want to kick back with something hip and contemporary.
That's my bag: sex, drugs, jazz/rock.

You were full of anxiety when you started reading this,
and now you're completely relaxed.
You're feeling tired but good, and very sleepy.
Your eyes are getting heavy.
You *need* to sleep (you want to let it all go and sleep)
and when you wake up you will love Communism.

I'll become famous as the first person to write a poem
that someone jerked off to.
Of course, who'd step forward and admit it.
This poem is dedicated
to you nuts out there who get hot reading poetry.

(Can you feature jerking off to a poem? Man, that's sick.)

POEM FOR EYDIE GORME

I have always secretly dug Eydie Gorme.
Ever since she sang on Steve Allen's old late-night show,
before she married Steve Lawrence who also sang on the show.
Eydie is a real fifties chick.
She dug Ahmad Jamal, shaved her belly,
had lots of cha-cha records in wrought-iron record stands.
Friday night she liked going to the neighborhood movie
where they advertised the candy counter during intermission.
She always invited you up for coffee
even if she didn't want to make it with you.

In 1999, Eydie's memoirs will be on the remaindered table
at Tro Harper's next to my Complete Works.
All Books On This Table — 90% Off.
"Oh look, Eydie Gorme's book, *Memoirs Of A Real Fifties Chick.*"
"Say, what's this? Have you ever heard of Eugene ('The Toe') Lesser?"
"Isn't he singing now with Fred Waring and the Pennsylvanians?"

CONSENTING ADULTS

"You're a now poet."
"You're an organic happening."
These are direct quotes.
Janet says I *look* like a great writer.
It's true. I look like a writer named Leonard Gold.
On the TV I hear this:
"Life can be a lot more than just a pretty face."
Now what the fuck does that mean?
There are probably two or three poets in the whole country
who write poems with a pencil, *without it being an affectation.*
This is the greatest poem I've ever written.
Or anyone else has ever written, for that matter.

We're up watching *Demetrius and the Gladiators.*
After a few commercials they start back in on an early reel,
and there we are watching the whole thing all over again.
Well, the movie's pretty good, but the second time in a row?
I get up and circumnavigate the channels only to realize
that *Demetrius and the Gladiators* the second time around
is the best thing on.

It's funny how an Elvis Presley movie
doesn't hold up when you're stoned.
"You don't have to buy a car, truck, or RV —
just come on down and have a cup of coffee with us."

Biographers will note that the TV was on a lot
while I wrote my poems.
My art is not lofty, you come to find out.
I'm just a nice guy on a good trip.
Mister Rogers for adults.

"Give me nookie or give me sleep."

"See the excitement of the Emmy Awards."

HELLO OUT THERE

I'm trying to give you peace of mind.
If you want it, you can have it right now.
Here it is. Peace of mind.

Alternate last lines:

Take it, shmuck.
Hi, my name is Lori.
You asked for it, you got it—western civilization.
I love you.
Thou still unravished bride of quietness.
Call 488-4650—easy lay.

YES, BUT IS IT GRAFFITI?

I'm sitting on the toilet writing a poem.
This poem. Writing these words that you're reading right now,
like "these words that you're reading right now." *Those* words.
If someone criticizes this poem on the grounds, for example,
that it's not a major work, you could always say,
"Yes, but he was on the toilet."
I'll match it, flawed though it might be,
with any poem in the same genre.
This is not the poem I sat down to write.
That was going to be the ultimate breakthrough (laxative imagery)
in the history of art, bunged up these many years.
Here I sit
broken-hearted.
Came to shit
but only farted.

SITTING ON THE TOILET

Sitting on the toilet rhymes with shitting on the toilet.
And that's exactly what I'm doing.
Actually, I'm shitting *in* the toilet.
Let me make that perfectly clear.
Writing is a tad anal-retentive, don't you think?
I'll be known in the 35th century only by this poem,
which will be in a famous anthology of scatological poems,
(entitled *Good Shit,* or *Boss Shit*).
Ah, a beautiful shit, speaking of shit, and not a bad poem either.
Talk about a poem not winning the Pulitzer Prize.

I like a good short poem.
Like a good short shit, it satisfies.

SUMMER SOLSTICE, 1971

This is my favorite day of the year.
The longest day, the most light, the first day of summer.
It's driving me fecund.
I worked my buns off today stacking aluminum in Sacramento.
Hot, Jim. Hundreds of degrees.
And the aluminum reflects the heat, you dig?
I'm relaxing now in the privacy of my own home,
smoking some boss pods and having
ten to twelve insights every second. For example:
I don't write poetry to get high, I write poetry to come down.
I was in a few bars up in Sacto on my lunch break.
Man, the town is full of these neo-Nazi bartenders.
I should get some cards printed up:
"I am Jewish. Later with the anti-Semitic remarks."
I was in an auto collision yesterday,
on one of those blind corners coming up Carson Road.
I was riding shotgun, reading the Sunday sports section.
My friend was visiting from Reno.
I should have told him to take those turns wide.
My head broke the windshield but I only got a small cut.
I could've died. But I didn't want to.
Not until September, at least.
I want to see my baby,
and I want to see the Giants win the pennant.
I hear that at around a hundred and twenty
you get a whole new set of teeth.
That's really something to shoot for.
Today, in this climax of light and self-knowledge,
I turn to the sun—the light, the Tao,
whatever you kids call it nowadays.
Life.

JUST A BOY AND HIS DOPE

I'm pulled over here by the back nine holes
of the San Geronimo Valley Golf Course and Country Club.
The cars are screaming past me.
I just bought a lid of grass for thirty-five dollars.
A car whizzes by me and actually shakes my Dodge truck
back and forth, and now even a VW is shaking my Dodge truck,
and I'm thinking I must be stoned, which I certainly am.
Thirty-five bucks sounded steep at first
but after a taste of the product I threw four tens on the table
and he gave me five singles back. Beautiful.
Maybe I *am* enlightened.
I've been working lately and today is payday.
I was looking for some primo shit and I found it, daddy.
I'm flipping, I guess. I never paid that much for a lid.
Wait a minute (stand-up comic motif), that was a Lambretta
that just shook my Dodge truck. (Big laugh here.)
I'm writing this on the back of mail received this morning.
Tim Tam Books, my pornography contact, sent me a brochure.
"Tim Tam has not forgotten you hardcore pocket book readers."
Ah, late Friday afternoon in the summer. After work. Really.
The question remains, as the cosmic and the mundane merge
on the horizon of my mind: Will the Giants ever get any pitching?

ON MY WAY TO WORK

Cruising down Carson Road (frankly, I'm ripped out of my gourd)
in my new used '64 International Travelall
(your basic mocha brown).
Me and a cop stop short at the blind fork at Madrone and Carson,
me with a little paranoid screech.
I gesture to him: You first, old bean.
He smiles and gestures back:
Don't be silly, my good man, after you.
Human contact flash. *The cop likes me.*
I resume driving down Carson Road with the cop behind me
and I don't feel paranoid anymore.
I'm thinking, this is groovy and light-hearted.
But it's much much heavier and farther out.
The cop loves me. And I love him.

Janet says, "It's a bit much."

ONA BLOSSOM

Janet says "a new father has been born."
This is my daughter's second day in the world.
The Giants are one game ahead with three to go.
We've all got a name, a time we were born, and a place.
The commonest thing is to have a baby, to be born.
Every second thousands of people are being born and dying.
That's the farthest out thing of all.
I do feel a closer bond between me and everyone else.
I could go on but I'm hip that you're hip.

JOHNNY MARIJUANASEED

"Poetry Says It Best!"
Motto of the Academy of American Poets' newsletter.

I always feel weird when I don't like a movie and someone else does.
I makes me think I'm a fascist intellectual.
In the third line here I've already got writer's cramp.
I'm going to Wyoming tomorrow for a couple of weeks
and so I'm up eating and drinking everything in the refrigerator.
I'm also putting together a platter of literary leftovers.
Stuff I couldn't work into any of my other poems,
if you really must know.
Watching *Lawrence of Arabia* with bad reception is like
(imagine here witty comparison).
If I were the greatest field-goal kicker of all time
I'd be known as Eugene "The Toe" Lesser.
If someone named Goldberg had invented the saxophone,
it would've been called a goldbergophone
(accent on the second syllable).
Wasn't William Holden great in *The Bridge On The River Kwai*?
Feminist radio station: KLIT.
I think that should just about wrap it up.
(What *are* dingleberries? — delete)

WORDS ARE HEAVY

I'm cranking them out tonight.
Next poem.

I DON'T HAVE A TOOTHACHE

What's to become of this poem?
What's to become of everyone and everything?

I don't have a toothache.
For this I'm grateful.
Thank you, Lord.

And what's to become of *us*?
We're all a bunch of greedy and/or uptight egomaniacs.
I'm not talking about the fat guys in socialist cartoons.
I'm talking about me and you, Jim.

Be that as it may (whatever that means),
what *I'm* into is just trying to accept
the simple yet overwhelming fact that at this moment
I do not have a toothache.
And neither does anyone else.
I was born for your sins (delete—irrelevant).

STOP THE WAR IN VIETNAM.

Remember, none of us has a toothache.
That's the main theme here.

WRITE IT DOWN

Me, Janet, and Marian are sitting at the table.
Janet and Marian are embroidering
and I am sporadically (and spasmodically) writing stuff down.
It's mellow, as Slim Gaillaird would say.
I go to the toilet (yes, right over to the toilet bowl)
and when I return I tell Janet and Marian that, while pissing,
I realized, as cashews swirled around in my mouth,
that the essential trip of eating is not to chew your food
and then swallow it, no, but to chew a little and let the food
melt over the tongue,
bathing the tongue with waves of pure pleasure,
like a hand caressing a cock.
Marian points to my open notebook and says, "Write it down."

ONA BY CANDLE LIGHT

1972

The Meaning And Purpose Of Life

Catchy title. ~~Woman libbing~~
What's the haps?
This poem is a front ~~for a candy store.~~
SEX.
Don't judge me.
~~I mean don't put me down.~~ (You can judge me anyway all you want)
~~Love me for your sake and love yourself for my sake.~~
DRUGS
A few more lines and this poem
will have a socially acceptable length..
~~Fifteen to twenty lines.~~
~~The poem is padding for the title.~~
~~Here are some more padded lines:~~
The meaning and purpose of life is what this poem's all about.
In case you ~~were thinking that~~ this was a piece of fluff.
I'll ~~just~~ tell you outright what the meaning and purpose of life is,
just to grandstand a little and prove to the skeptical
that I ~~know what everybody~~ do know what it is.
The meaning and purpose of life is (pretended drum roll)
(H-Bomb goes off, World Ends)
~~The text is corrupt at this point~~

Facsimile page from the original ms. (see p. 108).

JANUARY 17, 1972

A lot of times I think writing is weird.
But I'm fertile, I create.
There's nothing I can do about it.

My father would be 72 today.
After fifteen years I finally don't feel ripped off anymore.
According to statistics, he'd be dying soon, anyway.
I'll be 36 in June.
Half the age he would've been.
It's time I started stepping out.

Normally I would write, "I'm drinking a cup of Pero,"
but now it doesn't seem relevant.
It's a beautiful day outside and I'm inside, writing this.
That fact seems relevant.

John Berryman commits suicide.
Is that what poetry's all about?
(Imagine here several crossed out lines.)

I'm going outside.

MY RECORDS*

For a time I had my records arranged according to genre:
jazz, classical, rock, soul, folk, pop, country and western,
theater, Latin American, ethnic, spoken arts,
teen, and easy listening.
Then I arranged them alphabetically
(how hip can one human get?).
Tonight I've decided to re-arrange my records
according to randomness.

A thousand years from now
this will be the poem that is always anthologized.
Critics will agree that "My Records" is my greatest work.
The *Cleveland Plain Dealer* will call it "seminal . . .
the summit of his ouevre . . . a hip *Boewulf* . . ."

*This is considered the first truly modern poem,
 from which we date the earliest beginnings
 of post-technocratic poetry
 or roughly the period 1970–2155.

ODE TO JANET BROWN

George thought that the field goal should be eliminated.
But Jeff felt that if you eliminate the field goal
you also eliminate the fake field goal.
Janet pointed out, however, that the fake field goal
would not be eliminated; only the element of surprise
long associated with the fake field goal.

In the Bank of America I stood in line and paid the rent
while Janet stood in another line to get food stamps.
Later, she said, "The Bank of America giveth
and the Bank of America taketh away."

Tonight at dinner she said,
"A mediocre macaroni and cheese is the height of mediocrity."
Later, fooling around at the piano, I heard her say,
in the same voice she has for announcing
arrivals and departures at the airport,
"The song that asks the musical question, 'Why Was I Born?'"
On *Stormy Weather* she sang,
". . . since my man (or gal) and I ain't together."

Janet is pregnant and Jane the cat is pregnant.
So is the swordtail and the goldfish.
I'll be 35 when our baby is born in September.
Inside Janet's body there are two hearts beating.

It's three o'clock in the morning and it's raining.
She fell asleep with the embroidery book in her hand.
This is your no-frills love poem.

POEM INSPIRED BY ALAN DUGAN'S BIRTHDAY

Man, KJAZ isn't making it tonight.
Janet and I are babysitting for Susie.
I said I'd never write another poem like this.

Here's the Alan Dugan theme:
Every poem has some kind of not exactly
at one with nature vibe in it.
Because, as I said in an earlier work,
"art is ego, not scripture." Oh.
Nobody has ever written a poem
when everything was completely groovy.

Everybody's poems are heavy.
Everybody is heavy.
Everybody is also not heavy.

POEM INSPIRED BY ROBERT LOWELL'S BIRTHDAY

If Robert Lowell's birthday doesn't inspire me
then I'm a lost cause.
No, I'm very inspired by Robert Lowell's birthday.
I owe him a lot, he's a great poet, blah blah blah.
Let's face it, he's the best. Outside of me.
In my life, Robert Lowell is the road not taken.
You know, the intellectual psychoanalytic atheist angst booze trip.
I'm the only survivor of my generation.
They've all gone down the tubes.
Actually, I was first interested in Robert Lowell because
his last name also begins with an "L."
How about Jack Lemmon in "The Robert Lowell Story."
Small screen, black and white.
Yeah, because you are so fucking obscure.
Yevtushenko read at the College of Marin
and he drew thousands.
Posters all over Marin County: "Yevtushenko—Live at Olney Hall."
I don't know, maybe you're big nowadays.
Back East, or some shit.
I don't get out much.
I said what I wanted to say.

NOW IS THE TIME FOR ALL GOOD MEN TO COME

An obscenity evokes the image of genitals.
His or hers, as the case may be. Or both, in tandem.
Fuck is the biggie and cocksucker is up there.
Unless the word is in quotes. Then it's okay.
People who are uptight about the genitals don't want
anyone evoking an image of the genitals.
Then they are forced to look at the skin flick of their mind.
I, personally, am pro-genitals.
For those of you who don't mind or even enjoy
the occasional evoking of an image of genitals,
here are some words for you:
man
woman
love
guitar
doughnut
Coit Tower
Panama Canal
cosmos

STAND-UP READER

You're standing up in City Lights or some shit,
looking through my book for when I was born
so you can find out how many years you got on me.
You skim the poems looking for dirty parts,
or whatever your trip is: drugs, protest, the occult. Poetry.
I hope you don't get the wrong idea
when I say, "Fuck you, Jim."
I'm only kidding. Read and enjoy.
I love you.

OPEN LETTER TO RANDOLPH SCOTT

This title is just to catch the attention of
Randolph Scott freaks as they skim these pages,
looking for the dirty parts.
Your reward for stopping is this:
Thou still unravish'd bride of quietness.
Seriously, though, here's a little something for you:
Larry sucked her nipple while he played with her pussy.

SUPER YOGA

These lines are steps to heaven.
This poem will get you there,
if you will meet me half way,
on the paper where these words are written.
I can see you, looking up at you from this page.
This page is a one-way mirror for both of us.
Please think about this, but not too long.
Are you there yet?
I'm in no hurry to leave this poem, if you're not.
In fact, why not hang around a little.
Doodeedoodeedoo western civilization blah blah blah.
I think I'll blow one more chorus and then cut out.
(scat here twelve bars)

JOHNNY PUBERTY: DEEP DOWN I'M TWELVE YEARS OLD

Eugene Lesser, author of *Moby Dick, Hamlet, Beowulf,*
The New Testament, and *Three Jills In A Jeep,*
will speak this evening in the William Bendix Room
at the Hotel Decorator Tubs.
Your humble compiler of psychic lint
(Janet says I'm "puttering on the astral plane")
is quite wrecked, augmented by an outrageous
sixteen-ounce can of Colt 45.
I write down "Loving all things is where it's at,"
and then, after a minute or two, *I cross it out.*
If you can imagine that, then you're on a good empathy trip.
If you can imagine anything, you're doing all right.
Tonight I'm William Fucking Shakespeare.
I do it all.
Watch out, I'm dribbling downcourt now.
Fifty thousand people in the Astrodome are going apeshit
as the clock ticks down: four, three, two . . .
I start floating in from the foul line and end up
stuffing the ball through the hoop with both hands at the buzzer.
This wins the world's championship game in quadruple overtime
and breaks the all-time individual scoring record.
It also earns the right to fuck any three movie actresses in the world.

UNTITLED POEM, ATTRIBUTED TO WILLIAM SHAKESPEARE*

It's either turn off the light and stop writing
so I can keep the window open because it's over 100 degrees
here in Woodacre tonight (7/13/72 Bastille Eve),
or it's leave the light on so I can write this
and keep the window closed so that mosquitoes
and other large flying insects can't maraud
and buzz into the light bulb
and flick hysterically around the lampshade.

I decide to keep the window closed
and be hot and uncomfortable.
Why? So I can write the following:
I'm trying to get Robert Alda interested
in doing *The Mel Allen Story.*
This is what happens when you have
a couple reams of paper laying around.
If I were allotted only one scrap of paper once a year,
with a half-inch piece of Scripto lead,
you wouldn't see me writing stuff like
"They shall have been in-depth interviewed" or "Ed had edited it"
or *any* of this shit.

*This poem won Greatest Poem of the Geologic Era Award
in 7,000,000 A.D.

IT TAKES A HEAP O' LIVIN' TO BE A SIGMUND ROMBERG FREAK

Today (7/23/72) my high school sweetheart is 36.
Born on the same day as Don Drysdale.
Once we had a date back in high school
to go see *Gone With The Wind* in Bridgeport,
but when I arrived to pick her up
she got bugged because I hadn't shaved.
She said she wouldn't go to the movie with me if I wasn't shaved.
So what did I do? *I went home and shaved.*
The Fifties, man.
Remember the Gaylords?
Remember the hook shot?
Remember Eugene Lesser?
I like the Seventies. Nobody gives a shit.

MONDO WOODACRE

I'm up and around Susie's house looking for a ball point pen.
I realize I'm always a little pissed
when someone doesn't have anything to write with.
I mean when in the whole house there isn't a *pencil* even.
Suppose your life depends on writing something down.
I'm back where I began, in this chair, without a pencil even.
I think, forget it, you don't have to do any of this.
But no, I say: Liberate yourself.
Ask Susie for a pencil.
She says sure, her mind slightly blown by the request
because it means I want her to get up
from her comfy position on the couch.
She can't find one either, cruising all around the house,
looking in the same places I looked.
I think, could it all not be worth it?
Am I really supposed to write this down, or anything else?
At that moment, she finds a beat-up Bic-19 and flings it to me.
I'm writing and writing, not questioning it or myself.
I'm just about here when Jeff says, "Whatcha writin'?"
Here, Jeff, here it is.

LIFE IS A GAME OF INCHES

I'm turning on my new old 50¢ table console GE radio.
Old radios have to warm up.
"Life used to be full of transitions like that."—Janet Brown.
And then a few seconds later:
"Transistors eliminate transitions." (As told to Gerold Frank.)
Speaking of transitions, Diego Segui,
who just yesterday got traded from the A's to the Cardinals,
is here pitching today for the Cards in relief against the Giants.
The Giants were leading 4–1 but since I've turned the radio on
the Cards have scored four runs and nobody's out yet.
Segui takes a 6–4 lead going into the ninth
and pitches his third shutout inning,
setting the Giants down one-two-three to nail down the win.

This poem is destined for obscurity.
It has obscurity written all over it.
And so let me dedicate it to Diego Segui,
and to all of the good ones who never get any ink.

ONA IS ONE

I'm zenning out today.
Today I'm humble and obscure.
I like it so much I may do it again tomorrow.
Life is simple. It's so hard to write that.
You can almost break your fingers trying not to write it.
The truth is hiding in my mouth.
When Ona woke up today, Janet and I sang,
"Happy Birthday To You."
Now Ona can look back on her life like everyone else.
Life is one. Ona is one.

THE MEANING AND PURPOSE OF LIFE

Catchy title.
This poem isn't much on paper.
SEX.
What's the haps?
Don't judge me.
I mean, don't put me down.
You can judge me groovy all you want.
DRUGS.
A few more lines and this poem
will have a socially acceptable length.
The poem is padding for the title.
The meaning and purpose of life is what this poem's all about,
in case you were thinking that this was just a piece of fluff.
I'll just tell you outright what the meaning and purpose of life is,
just to grandstand a little and prove to the skeptical
that I really do know.
The meaning and purpose of life is
(H-bomb goes off. World ends.)

THE MINUTE WALTZ

Here I am holding off my daughter with my left arm
while writing this with my free hand.
This might cramp the style of some writers.
It's good for me. It gives me perspective.
I write only what is necessary.
I haven't got time for the ornaments.
She gives me about sixty seconds before making her move
for the ball point pen.
Here she comes, her fat little arms flailing.
(I must write this down.)
I'm holding off my daughter and writing.
Obviously, this can't go on much longer.
What do I need to write?
Here it is: Life is a precious gift.
Don't wait until you have cancer before you get hip to it.
She wants my pen. She fights the good fight.
But I persevere. Necessity drives me.
One more thing:[1]

[1]The text is corrupt at this point.

CROSSING RICHMOND BRIDGE ON THE NATCH

I'm driving across the Richmond Bridge and I'm not smoking a joint.
Close your eyes and try to imagine this.
I'm WBOD—Without Benefit of Drugs.
Trying to write this down, I veer in and out of my lane,
reaching everywhere for Bic pen and paper in the heavy traffic.
I wouldn't have done anything so obsessed if I were stoned.
I've tried recently to write poems on the natch. That's right.
It's really very interesting.
The fantastic consciousness of not being stoned.
I'll tell you, it's something else.
I know how I'm going to die:
Driving off the road trying to light a roach.
Or maybe while trying to write a poem on the Richmond Bridge
about not being stoned.
That would be fucking hilarious.

EUGENE "GENE" LESSER

Yes, that's me hitchhiking in the wind and rain
with my kid's laundry and some milk for a poor lactating mother.
The cars do not stop; they even pull away.
Talk about man's inhumanity to man.
Heads passing me by.
Marin sure ain't what it used to be.
Ah, remember the good old days in '68 and '69?
I'm hitting everyone with the one vibe
which is, briefly, *I need a ride.*
This is ego death. I'm saying, "Stranger, I need you."
They're saying, "No, I can't do it, I won't do it."
That's all right. No blame. I'm just a mirror. I love you.
You prick.
The question you have to ask yourself is:
Would you pick yourself up hitchhiking?

WHAT *IS* THE ELECTORAL COLLEGE?

Janet's going to vote. Maybe I'll vote, too.
I only voted one time, for LBJ in 1964.
Seriously, though, Goldwater was going to bomb the North.
EUGENE LESSER VOTES FOR LBJ
Someday this poem will have notes with it,
explaining what bombing the North meant,
what war it was, who LBJ and Goldwater were.
In three or four years.

We're reading the pamphlet with all the Propositions.
Proposition A is a statement of public policy
in Marin County requesting the President to begin
the total withdrawal of all U.S. troops from Southeast Asia.
I remember in 1964 picketing the Sheraton Plaza
where Madame Nhu was staying. END THE WAR IN SIXTY-FOUR.

The argument against the Proposition is written
by a group called SHAME, which stands for the committee to
Stop Helping America's Marxist Enemies.
The chairman of the board of the Bank of America,
who is *for* the Proposition, says:
"War is, as we would say in business, a low-yield operation."

Janet says, "The Democrats are the bad guys,
and the Republicans are the crazy guys."

JOHNNY FATHER: HERE AND NOW

Since I've had a kid my life has dramatically changed.
Used to be when I walked into a restuarant
I'd be thinking of man's inhumanity to man,
or the opening scene of my next novel,
or which three females in the restaurant I'd most like to screw.
But now I think: I hope this place has a high chair.

HUH?

Over the phone, Janet is talking to the Highway Patrolman
about a ticket on the Dodge truck for excessive smoke.
He wants the number of the ticket.
He says it's on the left.
She's got the ticket in her hand and she says
that there is no number on the left,
but there is a number on the right, if that's what he means.
He says to her: "Your right, the document's left."

BLOTTED OUT-NESS IS A FOUR-LETTER WORD

At first, you were really high and on top of it.
But here it is, one hundred reefers later, and you're totally wasted.
You can't move. You can't turn your head.
You're stoned, Jim. You're completely ripped.
Spaced.

Double spaced.

FIRST HALF

I'm listening to the 49ers–Chiefs game on the radio.
The Chiefs just went ahead, 10–3, on a Dawson–Taylor bomb.
7:40 remaining in the half.
Ona is waking up and starting to cry.
She wants to be in here, closer to the action.
A 54 yard field goal by Stenerud makes it 13–3, Chiefs,
and quiets down the crowd—
a rare Saturday night game at the 'Stick.
What my daughter really wants me to do
is go get her and walk around with her.
She knows I'm too sedentary and intellectual.
But I'm driven to write this poem (called "First Half").
I finally go get her and bring her back with me to the desk.
I know she's uncomfortable, dangling from my left arm,
but it's all working out, I'm able to write this down,
because she just got stoned out
staring *directly* into the flourescent lights
and forgot how uncomfortably I was dangling her,
and even that what she really wants
is for me to walk around with her.
Brodie to Kwalick, touchdown.
13–10, just before the half. All right.

1973

HEAVY PETTING
WATCHING *BANACEK*
SONG: *THEY SAY THAT BREAKING UP IS HARD TO DO*
MY TABLES: MEET IT IS I SET IT DOWN
CONSCIOUSNESS
SONG: *LAST GOODBYES*
THE DAY BEFORE THE READING
EUGENE AND ONA
TWENTY YEARS ON THE ROAD: FULL CIRCLE
SONG: *THERE'S A SPIRIT THAT'S MOVING ME*

"Eugene and Ona"

HEAVY PETTING

The bigger picture. This is always a good thing to think about.
Or even a good think to thing about.
Imagine, for example, that you are you.
That's one of my better lines. I'm just throwing them away here.
I'm after bigger game.
In a million years, people will call all of this,
(up through the 327th century) The Era of Early Man.
We're still a long way from Homo Groovus.
First, we have to get it together *with everybody*.
All of this so far has been Missing Link City.
In a million years, some high school kid will write a term paper called
4004 B.C.–3300 A.D.: Man In Embryo,
most of it lifted from an encyclopedia.
Yes, it may take us a long time (extra innings)
to get it together with everybody, what with western civilization, etc.
This piece of paper I'm writing on now
may be the only surviving specimen of this Era.
People will trip out on each word, that it might shed light
on the past, present, and future of mankind.
Well, those of you who read English (or whatever this is),
take what light from these words as you can.
Truth and Beauty did exist even at this late (early) date (1/28/73).
In fact, it was rampant. It wasn't all radioactive plastic.
The bigger picture, man. Not "man" as in "Got any papers, man,"
but as in Sir Ralph Richardson saying, "Pull yourself together, man."

WATCHING *BANACEK*

My father and mother were born in Poland and so I dig Banacek.
I love him.
Banacek has a phone in his car.
TV has infinite power of good or evil (but mostly evil).
In this episode it's revealed
that Banacek's father died several years ago.
"He was a good man."
Maybe I am Banacek. Or Hamlet, at least.
In a bar he says to the blonde,
"Do you always say no?"
"Usually," she says.
Janet says Banacek is a chauvinist pig.
"MCPsville."
We're smoking a Thai/hash oil bomber.
(Are there any drugs we haven't abused?)
Someday my poems will be dated
because of words like groovy, cosmic, and far out.
It would be just like my poems not to stand the test of time.
Let it be said, my name was writ on marijuana smoke.
Tonight I'm in a very subjunctive mood.
Poetry Mafia aside,
a poem's greatness is not in how it was written,
or what it says, but that it was written at all.
Let's hear it for bad poems and bad guys,
assholes, perverts, and male chauvinist pigs.
Yes, I'm up watching *Banacek*.
Which is more than I can say for William Fucking Shakespeare.
Hey, he's dead.
So dig me while you can.
I'm a National Monument.
One of a vanishing breed: People who are alive now.
I AM ALIVE NOW.
Yeah, dig me now and don't perturb my spirit with
eulogies, posthumous awards, and belated bullshit.

Don't go digging up my grave to prove who really wrote my poems.
"No one man could've encompassed so much."
Yeah, we all love dead people.
Because dead people can't love back.
Speaking of death and drugs, death must be the ultimate high
because we only get one hit of it. Per incarnation.
Death certainly is a cheap high.
Hey, God is not pitching a no-hitter.
God is pitching a perfect game.
To God I say, nolo contendere.
I never called my father by his name: Sigmund.
Your death is now outside the realm of personal sorrow
into the history of the world.
This poem rambles. But so what?
Take it like it is and be grateful.
Death is OK.
It's like ending a poem.
Groovy, cosmic, and far out.

THEY SAY

Dm
They say that break-ing up is for-
" " "
love can't last
Bb
hard to do but I know one
-ev- er but I could nev-
Dm
Bb
- thing that is hard- er.
- er ac-cept it.
Dm C Bb
It's be-ing with the one you love when the one you love don't
I've got some grow-ing up to do and for this, girl, I
A7 Dm
love you No mat-ter the time or space be-tween
thank you
A Dm
us. I'll al-ways rec-ol-
Bb
lect your touch.

Dm
I'll take to heart the words you told me ___.
C
when you said I loved ___ you
A7   Dm
too much ___________ They say that
Bb
all of this is make ___ be-lieve
Dm   Bb
and it will one ___ day be for-got- ________ ten
Dm   C
The on-ly thing I know that's true ___
Bb   A7
is ___ it was good to love you ___   love you for a-
Dm   Bb
-while __________

MY TABLES: MEET IT IS I SET IT DOWN

Dick Cavett is talking to someone about marijuana.
Dick admits that certain activities can be enhanced
by smoking marijuana—listening to records, etc. —
but says that "no important work" can be done on grass.
For example, he says he couldn't imagine writing while stoned.
Funny, I can imagine it. If I close my eyes real hard.

CONSCIOUSNESS

Think of all the generations and eras of mankind.
And realize that we, you and I, are alive at the same time,
and not only alive at the same time,
but that I'm writing this and you're reading it.
I'm watching "Invasion Earth—2150 A.D." with Peter Cushing.
He invents a time machine (suspension of disbelief here).
He can be in the future or in the past.
Sure, it's easy to be in the future or in the past,
but what about the now. There's the rub, to quote Mel Friedman.
(*The future is the past in drag.*
There's a line I would've left in in 1968.)
And when you read this in 2150 A.D.
we will share the same now as we do now.
That's what poetry is all about, baby.
On the other hand, this may not hold up next week,
let alone centuries from now.
In fact, no one may ever read this except me,
and even I may never read it after writing it down tonight.
Or maybe it will become one of the great all-time classics,
along with the Bible, the works of Shakespeare,
and *Consciousness Made Simple* by Ernest F. Hackett.

LAST GOODBYES

F7/Eb
D7
Gm9
I'll sing this song for both of us I know you feel it, too
Bbm7
Yes I know you do. But I
F
Am/E
F7/Eb
know where you're at I nev-er knew that a day would come and we'd be through
D7
Gm9
so these are my last good - byes as the
Bbm7
mu - sic dies

THE DAY BEFORE THE READING

Thought #1: What does it all mean?
Second thought: What does any part of it mean?
I shouldn't have eaten that sandwich.
Am I really going to stand up in front of people
and read my poems?
That sounds at least as scary as going to the dentist.
Or having a bar mitzvah.
Yes, this poetry reading is a chance to recoup my lost bar mitzvah,
which I blew and the whole world blew.
I had to memorize all this stuff,
and the Hebrew I read was all spelled out phonetically.
It was a fraud, Jim.
Unlike my bar mitzvah consciousness,
I want to create an original work for the reading,
but even if I do
it'll be ancient fucking history by tomorrow at 2 p.m.
The only truly original thing I can do tomorrow is show up.
Showing up always has a lot going for it.
Today I am a ball point pen.
On the day before the reading
I am the far out poet that you want me to be.
I notice the shadows of birds, the sun on the grass.
I see it all. And so do you.
I'm making all this up.

EUGENE AND ONA

Me and my daughter are hanging out at my place tonight.
We're eating now.
She puts her foot in the soup. I frown.
My cuff, however, is in my own soup
as I reach across to write this down.
We're having a mellow dinner together.
My daughter loves to be ignored while she eats, and so do I.
I don't mind if you talk to me while I eat.
In fact, I enjoy it,
as long as I don't have to look at you. Or say anything.
We're eating my split pea soup (with barley).
Ona picks up a cracker and looks at it
with intense awe and delight.
She doesn't know it's just a cracker.
I tell her it's not cool to throw food on the floor.
She looks at me as though to say, "Oh, really?"
Ona is entering the supposed and so-called terrible twos.
I myself am deep into the terrible thirty-sixes.
I try to emulate Ona.
To do my best, to do what I want,
to love openly, to live in the now,
and a few other biggies.
Someday I will be me.
And someday Ona will be Ona all over again.
This split pea soup is great.
Would you like a bowl?

TWENTY YEARS ON THE ROAD: FULL CIRCLE

Thou still unravish'd bride of quietness.
Thou foster child of silence and slow time.
Seriously, though, I've always loved poetry.
It's so neat. If you don't get hung up on semantics.
The first poem I ever wrote was a sonnet, an imitation of Keats.
I was seventeen. Here's the first line,
the first line of poetry I ever wrote:
"The clock ticks on with my thoughts in silent pursuit."
Talk about not showing early flashes of genius.
I've been a late bloomer in this life.
I started coming on strong after thirty.
This poem is an attempt to create truth and beauty.
I'm writing it instead of watching the UCLA–Cal basketball game.
I notice it's fourteen lines like my first one.

There's A Spirit That's Moving Me

F
F#°
Good-bye need   good-bye greed
C   C7   F
good-bye to strug-gle 'n' strife ____   Now I'm free
F#°   G7
I love me   oh where have I been all of my life ______
C7   F7
I wish that I could   tell you e-nough
C7   G7
try it your-self and you'll see ______
C   E7   Am   D7
I used to stoop __   now my shoul-ders nev-er droop cause there's a
C   G7   C
spir-it that's mov-ing me ______

This book was designed and produced by Michael Sykes and Cindy Ohama at their home in Inverness, California. The text was set in Futura Book and Italic by Michael Sykes. One thousand copies were printed by Thomson-Shore, Inc. in the summer of 1985.

*The author (left) with his editor and publisher, Michael Sykes.
Photo by Ed Buryn—Fairfax, California, circa 1980.*

Peter Wild, *Barn Fires*
    32 pp, perfectbound, $3.00
Frank Graziano, *Desemboque*
    48 pp, perfectbound, $4.00
Christine Zawadiwsky, *Sleeping With The Enemy*
    32 pp, perfectbound, $4.00
Jeffery Beam, *The Golden Legend*
    48 pp, perfectbound, $5.00
David Hilton, *Penguins*
    24 pp, hand-sewn, $3.00
Joanne Kyger, *Up My Coast*
    24 pp, hand-sewn, $3.00
Frank Stewart, *The Open Water*
    64 pp, perfectbound, $5.00
Arthur Sze, *Dazzled*
    60 pp, perfectbound, $5.00
John Brandi, *The Cowboy from Phantom Banks*
    80 pp, smythe-sewn, $6.95
Peter Wild, *The Light on Little Mormon Lake*
    32 pp, hand-sewn, $4.00
Kirk Robertson, *Two Weeks Off*
    48 pp, hand-sewn, $5.00
Norbert Krapf, *Circus Songs*
    32 pp, hand-sewn, $4.00
Cole Swensen, *It's Alive She Says*
    88 pp, smythe-sewn, $5.00
Joan Wolf, *The Divided Sphere*
    96 pp, smythe-sewn, $5.00
Michael Conway, *The Odyssey Singer*
    88 pp, smythe-sewn, $5.00

Floating Island I
    120 pp, smythe-sewn, $6.95
Floating Island II
    184 pp, perfectbound, $8.95
Floating Island III
    160 pp, perfectbound, $12.95